CONTENTS

INTRODUCTION

From the earliest times, people have had ideas and tried to make them work. If nothing had ever been invented, we would still be living in caves, and going to sleep as soon as it was dark. Think of discoveries and inventions like electricity, television, cars and computers. It is difficult to imagine life without them. But sometimes inventions just seem crazy, and this book is about that sort of invention. Our choices are rated according to:

MOTIVE

Here, we looked at the reason why something was invented. In many cases, it was because the inventor wanted to achieve something, but could not find the right equipment. Very often, it involved trying to break a world record. That's something else about people: they have always wanted to go higher, or faster, or deeper, or further than anybody else has ever gone before.

NO.7 | BOWLINGUAL TRANSLATOR

The BowLingual was developed by Japanese toy company Takara. A microphone attached to the dog's collar picks up the sounds it makes and transmits them to a hand-held receiver. They are run through a "doggy mood" **database** to find the closest match. A screen displays the results using both words and graphics!

MOTIVE
This gadget was developed to help dog owners to understand what their pets mean, so they can get to know their best friends better.

CRAZY FACTOR
You'd have to be pretty crazy to follow dogs around with a microphone, like the animal experts who helped to create the database in this gadget.

FEATURES
A wireless microphone transmits sounds made by the dog. The dog's type and size are logged in, and then the receiver **analyses** the sounds. It works out the **emotional** state the dog is in from a choice of six, and compares them to a database that contains about 200 "translation patterns".

CRAZY FACTOR 9/10

For this category, we looked at things including how useful the invention would be, and whether it seemed sensible or silly. People laughed at lots of different things when they were first invented, including aeroplanes, radio and mobile phones. But people often change their minds, and nobody laughs at those things now. They are just part of everyday life.

FEATURES 5/10

This is the practical section. It covers all the different parts of the invention and explains what they are for. Details like speed, the materials used to make it, its size, weight and the type of fuel it needs will also be included here.

UTILITY 4/10

In this section, we give a score that is based on how useful the invention is or will be. This is not always easy to say. It is often best to wait for a while, try out the invention, and then decide. Then, it might be difficult to see how anyone ever managed without it!

VALUE 2/10

This score looks at the price of the invention and whether it was worth what it cost to develop. The first version of an invention is called a prototype. A prototype may be very expensive. But later, it may be possible to mass-produce the invention, perhaps in a factory. Then, the price usually goes down – sometimes quite dramatically.

Results include phrases like: "I want to go out" or "Come on, play with me."

UTILITY

Dog owners may think they know what their pet means, but this is a fun way to check. If you want to see happy words and faces on the screen, give your pet good food, attention and lots of walks.

VALUE

If you're animal-crazy, you may be willing to hand over about £64 for this gadget.

The Dog Translator translates the barks of our dogs and converts them into plain English.

EXTREME SCORES

This is a lot of fun, and may help you to communicate better with your pet.

MOTIVE 5/10
CRAZY FACTOR 9/10
FEATURES 5/10
UTILITY 4/10
VALUE 2/10
= TOTAL SCORE 25/50

This remarkable miniature submarine lets you see what is lurking in the depths of the ocean, without going underwater! Nigel Jagger and his company H2Eye spent ten years developing the tiny machine, which works by remote control. It has an on-board camera which sends images to a video screen above the surface.

MOTIVE

Nigel Jagger wanted to develop an easier way to explore beneath the sea. He was inspired by Jules Verne's exciting book about underwater exploration, *20,000 Leagues Under the Sea.*

CRAZY FACTOR

You can sit in a boat up above and watch what is happening below, without struggling into a diving suit.

FEATURES

The Spyfish runs on batteries and is fitted with **floodlights** and cameras. It is fully computerized, easy to operate, and no diving ability is necessary!

The Mini Sub is a gadget that allows everyone to explore the deep sea without diving into it.

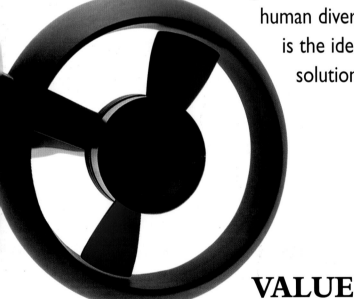

The Mini Sub is powered by batteries.

UTILITY

Spyfish lets people of any age or ability explore the oceans of the world in comfort and safety. When conditions are too cold or dangerous for a human diver, it is the ideal solution.

VALUE

This remarkable deep-sea experience costs about £7,925 – not really a rock-bottom price but a unique way to explore the sea.

If you fancy a virtual underwater diving experience – and you have enough money – this is the machine for you.

MOTIVE
3/10

CRAZY FACTOR
3/10

FEATURES
3/10

UTILITY
3/10

VALUE
4/10

= TOTAL SCORE

16/50

Icy Rider is a pedal cycle with a difference – it even works on snow and ice! Adventurer Doug Stoup, who was the first American to ski across country from the Antarctic coast to the South Pole, came up with the idea, working with designer and engineer Dan Hanebrink.

MOTIVE

Doug Stoup decided that skiing was too slow, so he came up with the idea for a pedal cycle that would work in all conditions.

CRAZY FACTOR

Imagine being able to cycle where no mountain biker would dare to go! With this bike, you could even give cross-country skiers the slip!

FEATURES

Icy Rider has a long **wheelbase** that gives the bike stability. Massive tyres provide superb traction. It is made without any plastic parts because they would freeze and shatter in low temperatures.

The tyres of the Icy Rider are superfat.

UTILITY

One of the best things about this machine is that it is very easy to **manoeuvre**. It can be used on any surface – not just snow and ice – and in all conditions. It is worked by pedals, just like a bike, so there is no engine to break down.

VALUE

If you thought pedal power was cheap, think again! This easy rider costs a cool £2,530 but will let you go anywhere you want.

The Icy Rider is an extreme terrain bike capable of riding fast on icy plains and mountains.

If you love adventure, you'll be guaranteed an incredible journey on this **all-terrain** machine.

MOTIVE
4/10

CRAZY FACTOR
8/10

FEATURES
4/10

UTILITY
4/10

VALUE
3/10

= TOTAL SCORE
23/50

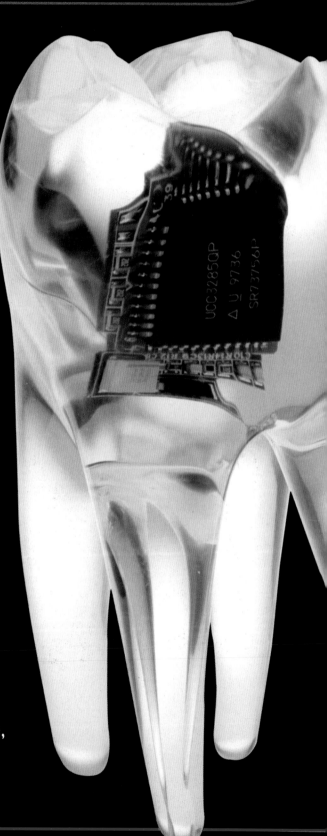

This invention sounds like something out of a James Bond film, but it could soon be a reality. The tiny phone that fits inside a tooth was developed by students James Auger and Jimmy Loizeau. These brilliant young inventors believe that one day surgeons will regularly be asked to implant tiny devices like this that can receive calls from mobile phones and radios.

MOTIVE

These young inventors wanted to make people think about the computer technology of the future. They also wanted to investigate the possible effects of in-body technology.

CRAZY FACTOR

This one really is crazy. Despite the convenience, you might feel a bit crazy if one of your teeth started to talk to you!

Implant inventors Jimmy Loizeau (left) and James Auger.

FEATURES

The tiny phone is designed to be fitted into a molar by a dentist. It will use a radio receiver to pick up signals, and a **vibrating** plate to send them as sounds along the jawbone to the ear.

UTILITY

This gadget is still being developed, and a lot more work is needed. There are no plans yet for it to be able to make calls. Secret agents might think it is a dream come true, however!

VALUE

Never mind toothache – at a whopping £14,900 plus a visit to the dentist, the price could give you a headache.

The Phone Tooth is a small chip attached to our tooth. It is capable of receiving phone signals.

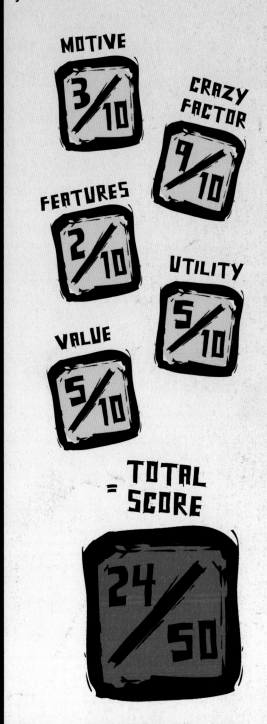

EXTREME SCORES

This one may be for you if you can't be bothered to carry your mobile phone – or if your name's Bond, James Bond.

MOTIVE
3/10

CRAZY FACTOR
9/10

FEATURES
2/10

UTILITY
5/10

VALUE
5/10

= TOTAL SCORE
24/50

The BowLingual was developed by Japanese toy company Takara. A microphone attached to the dog's collar picks up the sounds it makes and transmits them to a hand-held receiver. They are run through a "doggy mood" **database** to find the closest match. A screen displays the results using both words and graphics!

MOTIVE

This gadget was developed to help dog owners to understand what their pets mean, so they can get to know their best friends better.

CRAZY FACTOR

You'd have to be pretty crazy to follow dogs around with a microphone, like the animal experts who helped to create the database in this gadget.

FEATURES

A wireless microphone transmits sounds made by the dog. The dog's type and size are logged in, and then the receiver **analyses** the sounds. It works out the **emotional** state the dog is in from a choice of six, and compares them to a database that contains about 200 "translation patterns".

Results include phrases like: "I want to go out" or "Come on, play with me."

UTILITY

Dog owners may think they know what their pet means, but this is a fun way to check. If you want to see happy words and faces on the screen, give your pet good food, attention and lots of walks.

VALUE

If you're animal-crazy, you may be willing to hand over about £64 for this gadget.

The Dog Translator translates the barks of our dogs and converts them into plain English.

This is a lot of fun, and may help you to communicate better with your pet.

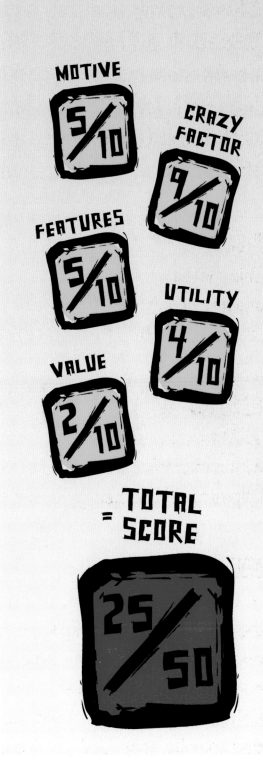

MOTIVE
5/10

CRAZY FACTOR
9/10

FEATURES
5/10

UTILITY
4/10

VALUE
2/10

= TOTAL SCORE
25/50

This clever device converts finger movements into text. Ryan Patterson, a 17-year-old US student, invented it after he saw deaf people ordering food in a restaurant. He was inspired by Braille, a system that lets blind people "read" with their fingertips. He wired a leather glove with sensors to pick up hand movements.

MOTIVE

To help deaf people who use sign language to be more independent. Using the glove could mean that they do not have to rely so much on interpreters.

CRAZY FACTOR

Imagine having to wear a leather glove wired with electronic equipment in all weathers, just to tell people what you want!

FEATURES

A soft leather golf glove is fitted with ten sensors and a **transmitter**. A monitor on the back of the glove **interpret** the movements using a specially-designed computer programme. A tiny screen displays them as text.

The Braille
Glove contains
a transmitter
and a moniter.

This invention might not be as crazy
as it looks if it improves the lives of
millions of deaf people.

UTILITY

This smart glove translates deaf
people's finger movements into text.
It means they do not have to write
down what they want, or rely on sign
language interpreters. It could help
millions of deaf
people across
the world.

VALUE

The gadget has not reached the
shops yet, but it may cost around
about £80.

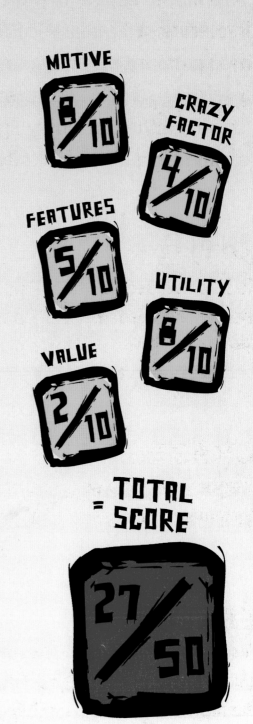

MOTIVE
8/10

CRAZY
FACTOR
4/10

FEATURES
5/10

UTILITY
8/10

VALUE
2/10

= TOTAL
SCORE

27/50

The Braille Glove understands the gestures
and sign language of the deaf people and
translates them into text.

This device uses a laser beam to project a virtual keyboard – a glowing red outline – on to a flat surface. **A sensor** monitors the reflection and works out which "keys" are being struck. The keyboard can be used with lots of devices including laptops, palm-held computers and mobile phones.

MOTIVE

To make it easier to input data to mobile and wireless devices, which have very small keyboards that are often difficult to use.

CRAZY FACTOR

This amazing keyboard isn't really there, but it behaves just like a real keyboard. It even makes realistic tapping sounds!

FEATURES

The keyboard is battery-operated and is small enough to fit into a pocket. It uses infra-red and laser technology to project a full-size QWERTY (standard) keyboard.

The laser beam unit is the size of a chocolate bar.

UTILITY

This virtual keyboard is a comfortable and convenient way to enter data into all kinds of mobile devices. It is simple to use, and it really does work.

VALUE

The first model cost more than most computers at about £26,600, but the price has already fallen to about £106.

The virtual keyboard can be projected on to any flat surface with the help of laser beam.

EXTREME SCORES

This clever device really shrinks the size of a computer – you can carry a full-size keyboard in your pocket.

MOTIVE 8/10

CRAZY FACTOR 9/10

FEATURES 6/10

UTILITY 6/10

VALUE 6/10

= TOTAL SCORE 35/50

The **Gibbs Aquada** looks like an ordinary car, except that the steering wheel is in the centre of the dashboard. But its average looks hide a big secret – it is actually an amphibious vehicle that works on land and water. Drive up to the water's edge, and it will convert to a boat at the flick of a switch.

MOTIVE

To produce an efficient and practical high-speed amphibious vehicle that looks and drives just like an ordinary car.

FEATURES

The Aquada's jet-propulsion system generates almost a ton of thrust. Operate it as you enter the water, and the wheels will tuck away into its body in just 12 seconds.

CRAZY FACTOR

Is it a car? Is it a boat? No, it's both. Imagine not having to find a bridge when you want to cross a river – that's really crazy.

The Gibbs Aquada can reach a speed of 100 mph on land, and 30 mph on water.

The wheels of the **Gibbs Aquada** rise up into the body to become a boat while entering water.

UTILITY

This vehicle performs well on both land and water. It might help you to dodge traffic jams, as long as there is a suitable stretch of water nearby.

VALUE

The Gibbs Aquada is available now for about £132,000. For that, you could buy a great boat and an amazing sports car.

EXTREME SCORES

This crazy vehicle is for the man or woman who has everything, plus plenty of cash to spend on grown-up toys.

MOTIVE
7/10

CRAZY FACTOR
7/10

FEATURES
8/10

UTILITY
8/10

VALUE
8/10

= TOTAL SCORE
38/50

Americans Paul Moller and Michael Moshier have invented two flying machines. Solotrek is a one-man flying machine and Skycar, a car-like vehicle, is designed to take driver and a passenger through the air. These strange vehicles may be the future of travel.

MOTIVE

To develop a "personal" flying machine that could take off from the roof of a house; to make everyday flight **accessible** to everyone.

CRAZY FACTOR

Skycar has been in development for 40 years and has cost about £106 million so far. Despite years of investment, neither vehicle has flown for more than a few seconds.

Solotrek and Skycar are the solo flying machine.

Skycar can reach a top speed of 350 mph.

FEATURES

Solotrek has two large metal fans powered by gas engines. The pilot stands on footrests, straps on a body belt and steers using a joystick. Skycar has eight 150 horsepower engines and may reach speeds of up to 350mph.

UTILITY

These inventions will get off the ground - eventually. Taking to the skies might be a way to avoid traffic jams in the future – until the skies become just as crowded.

VALUE

These fantastic machines will not be cheap, and if they ever go on sale may cost anything from £42,500.

Forget the garage – the vehicle of the future could be kept on a rooftop parking pad.

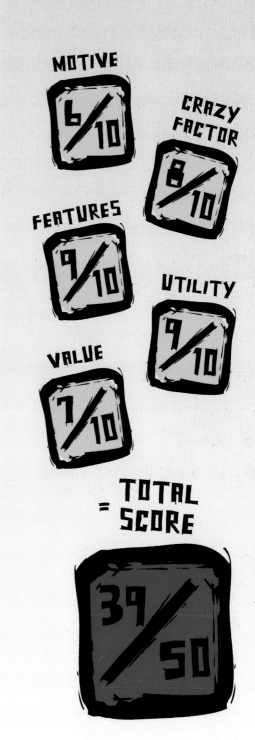

MOTIVE 6/10

CRAZY FACTOR 8/10

FEATURES 9/10

UTILITY 9/10

VALUE 7/10

= TOTAL SCORE 39/50

This weird-looking vehicle is being developed by **US** car giant **General Motors.** It needs no fuel and produces no pollution. There is no engine, no steering column and no brake pedal, so you can see right through the front. Hy-Wire is powered by a chemical reaction that generates only heat and a small amount of water.

MOTIVE

To design a vehicle that does not run on fossil fuels – and that could help to solve many of the world's **environmental** problems.

CRAZY FACTOR

There is no steering column, which means that you can steer from anywhere inside this vehicle. It is perfect for back-seat drivers!

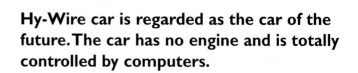

Hy-Wire car is regarded as the car of the future. The car has no engine and is totally controlled by computers.

Hy-Wire has no steering columns and no brake pedal.

FEATURES

The Hy-Wire is steered electronically using two small handgrips that incorporate the brakes. There is no rear-view mirror; instead, a camera projects an image of the road behind.

UTILITY

The vehicle is powered by fuel cells similar to those used in space technology. It costs nothing to run and gives off no pollution.

VALUE

This amazing car will not be cheap, and the first models available may cost about £1.9 million.

EXTREME SCORES

This car does not need fuel, so it could be the answer to many **environmental** problems.

MOTIVE
9/10

CRAZY FACTOR
5/10

FEATURES
10/10

UTILITY
10/10

VALUE
9/10

= TOTAL SCORE
43/50

NO.1

EARTH SIMULATOR

This incredible invention is the world's most powerful **supercomputer**. Developed by Japanese scientists in 2002, they built the Earth **Simulator**, a massive machine that can monitor everything in the world, from the depths of the sea to the top of the highest mountain. It has already processed data to predict the world's climate for the next 50 years.

MOTIVE

To create a machine that can simulate conditions on Earth, and help scientists to predict the future of the planet.

CRAZY FACTOR

You'd have to be crazy to want to re-create the Earth. Even crazier is the fact that it has actually been done!

FEATURES

The Earth Simulator is the world's fastest supercomputer. It is more powerful than the 12 next-fastest supercomputers put together, and covers an area the size of four tennis courts. It is connected using 1,750 miles of cable, and can perform 35 trillion calculations per second.

The Earth Simulator is as big as the size of four tennis court.

VALUE

You would need to dig deep into your pockets to find the £186 million cost of this project – but it's worth every penny. You can't put a price on helping to save the planet.

The Earth Simulator is the fastest supercomputer ever built.

UTILITY

This machine will help with essential research into the Earth's **environment**. Scientists will be able to plug in data gathered from all over the world, and use it to predict the future. It will also help to show whether special environmental policies will produce the desired effect.

EXTREME SCORES

This has to be the craziest, the most amazing, and also the most important invention of all time.

MOTIVE 10/10

CRAZY FACTOR 10/10

FEATURES 8/10

UTILITY 9/10

VALUE 10/10

= TOTAL SCORE 47/50

Choosing just ten inventions for this book was very difficult.
Here are five mad inventions that didn't quite make the final list...

SPUTMIK MICROPHONE

The Sputmik wireless microphone is a fun way for
everyone to be heard. The size of a
basketball, it is easy to handle and padded
for safety. It can be handed from person to
person, passed overhead or even thrown like a
ball. Sputmik was developed by the
Massachusetts Institute of Technology (MIT)
and Design Continuum of Boston, US.

SHOP 2000

This new-generation **vending machine**
invented by Hettie Herzog stocks up to 200
different essential items and keeps
perishable goods cool. It delivers goods
using a robotic arm, produces a receipt, and
even gives you a bag if you want one. The
Shop 2000 is 4.4 metres wide and takes
cash or credit cards.

WHEELMAN

Grant Taylor and design engineer Muzza Grant have spent 20 years working on this mad gadget which they bill as the latest way to travel. It looks like a miniature motorbike and works a bit like a motorised skateboard. It is steered using body weight, and a hand-held **throttle** regulates the speed. Wheelman is available now for about £475.

SMART SKIS

When you go skiing, why not think with your feet for a change? These smart skis from Head think for you. They use special material that responds to pressure and movement by generating electricity. Computer chips in the skis monitor this, then estimate snow condition and how hard you are turning. The information is fed back to the skis, which relax or stiffen automatically to provide a smoother ride. The cost is about £500.

CINDY SMART DOLL

This almost-living doll takes interactive play to a new level. She can read flash cards, do simple sums and recognise shapes and colours. She uses her vocabulary of 650 words – plus a little German, Spanish, Italian and French – to answer 70 different pre-programmed questions. Working parts include two 16-bit **microprocessors**, voice-recognition software and a digital camera.

STATS

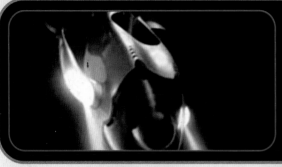

NO. 10 SPYFISH MINI SUB

		Extreme Scores	
Country:	UK	Extreme Scores	
Year:	2003	Motive	3
Inventor:	Nigel Jagger	Crazy Factor	3
Company:	H²EYE	Features	3
Power Source:	Battery	Utility	3
Cost:	£7925	Value	4

TOTAL SCORE 16/50

NO. 9 ICY RIDER

		Extreme Scores	
Country:	US	Extreme Scores	
Year:	2003	Motive	4
Inventor:	Doug Stoup	Crazy Factor	8
Company:	Hanebrink	Features	4
Power Source:	pedals	Utility	4
Cost:	£1,860	Value	3

TOTAL SCORE 23/50

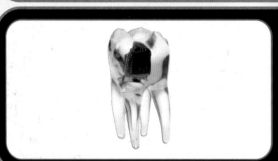

NO. 8 PHONE TOOTH

		Extreme Scores	
Country:	UK	Extreme Scores	
Year:	2002	Motive	3
Inventor:	James Auger/Jimmy Loizeau	Crazy Factor	9
Company:	non yet	Features	2
Power Source:	non-working model	Utility	5
Cost:	£14,900	Value	5

TOTAL SCORE 24/50

NO. 7 BOWLINGUAL DOG TRANSLATOR

		Extreme Scores	
Country:	Japan	Extreme Scores	
Year:	2003	Motive	5
Inventor:	Dr. Norio Kogure	Crazy Factor	9
Company:	Takara	Features	5
Power Source:	battery	Utility	4
Cost:	£64	Value	2

TOTAL SCORE 25/50

NO. 6 SIGN LANGUAGE TRANSLATOR GLOVE

		Extreme Scores	
Country:	US	Extreme Scores	
Year:	2004	Motive	8
Inventor:	Ryan Patterson	Crazy Factor	4
Company:	none as yet	Features	5
Power Source:	battery	Utility	8
Cost:	still in development	Value	2

TOTAL SCORE 35/50

NO. 5 VIRTUAL KEYBOARD

Country:	US	Extreme Scores	
Year:	2003	Motive	8
Inventor:	Canesta	Crazy Factor	9
Company:	VKB	Features	6
Power Source:	battery	Utility	6
Cost:	£106	Value	6

TOTAL SCORE 35/50

NO. 4 GIBBS AQUADA

Country:	UK	Extreme Scores	
Year:	2003	Motive	7
Inventor:	Peter Gibbs	Crazy Factor	7
Company:	Gibbs Technologies	Features	8
Power Source:	jet propulsion	Utility	8
Cost:	£132,000	Value	8

TOTAL SCORE 38/50

NO. 3 SOLOTREK/SKY CAR

Country:	US	Extreme Scores	
Year:	Still in development	Motive	6
Inventor:	Paul Moller/Michael Moshier	Crazy Factor	8
Company:	none as yet	Features	9
Power Source:	Solotrek , gas-powered fans; Skycar, 8 x 150hp engines	Utility	9
		Value	7
Cost:	$250,000/£132,000		

TOTAL SCORE 39/50

NO. 2 HY-WIRE CAR

Country:	US	Extreme Scores	
Year:	Still in development	Motive	9
Inventor:	Paul MacCready	Crazy Factor	5
Power Source:	electrochemical reaction	Features	10
Company:	General Motors	Utility	10
Cost:	Up to /£1.9 million	Value	9

TOTAL SCORE 43/50

NO. 1 EARTH SIMULATOR

Country:	Japan	Extreme Scores	
Year:	2002	Motive	10
Inventor:	various	Crazy Factor	10
Company:	various	Features	8
Power Source:	electricity	Utility	9
Cost:	$350 million	Value	10

TOTAL SCORE 43/50

ACCESSIBLE within easy reach

ALL-TERRAIN able to travel over any ground

ANALYSE work out the cause of something

DATABASE a collection of information, especially in a computer

EMOTIONAL showing strong feeling

ENVIRONMENT surroundings, especially of the Earth

FLOODLIGHT unit producing a beam of intense light

INTERPRET explain information

LEAGUE a class or category

MANOEUVRE a movement or action

MICROPROCESSOR a small circuit that deals with information in a computer

POLLUTION poisonous or harmful substances in the air, especially caused by burning fuel such as coal or petrol

PROTOTYPE one of the first units made of an invention, which is often changed before the final version goes into production

REACTION an event that takes place as a result of another action

SENSOR something that receives a signal and responds to it

SIMULATOR a machine that reproduces certain conditions, especially when carrying out experiments

SUPERCOMPUTER term for one of the fastest computers available.

TERRAIN ground or a piece of ground, especially with reference to the type of ground

THROTTLE a device that controls the levels of fuel, or fuel and air mixture that enters and engine

TRANSMITTER equipment that is used for sending signals or messages

VENDING MACHINE a machine that dispenses goods when a coin or card is inserted

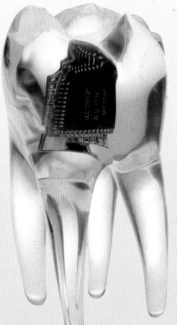

VIBRATING producing a slight, rapid and regular shaking

WHEELBASE distance from the centre of the front wheel to that of the rear wheel